W9-BKM-965

PING READER
LEVEL 2
250-750 WORDS

Itty-Bitty Animals

by Joan Emerson

Scholastic Inc.

PHOTO CREDITS: Front cover: Thinkstock (RF); back cover: Christophe Lehenaff/Getty Images; title page: iStockphoto; 4: Momo5287/Shutterstock; 5: iStockphoto; 6: hagit berkovich/Shutterstock; 7: hagit berkovich/Shutterstock; 9: Merlin D Tutle/Getty Images; 10: Jared Hobbs/Getty Images; 11: Ronnie Howard/Shutterstock; 13: Tom Hacker/Loveland Daily Reporter-Herald/AP Photo; 14: poeticpenguin/Shutterstock; 15: poeticpenguin/Shutterstock; 17: Liu Jian/Xinhua Press/Corbis; 18: Michel Gunther/Photo Researchers, Inc.; 19: Fanny Reno/Shutterstock; 20: Kristin Snodgrass of www.MyLittleSheep.com; 21: Alexey Stiop/Shutterstock; 22: Sandesh Kadur/NPL/Minden Pictures; 23: Tom McHugh/Getty Images; 25: Bebeto Matthews/AP Photo; 26: Daniel Wilson/Shutterstock; 27: Dennis Donohue/Shutterstock; 28:Christophe Lehenaff/Getty Images; 29: iStockphoto; 30: iStockphoto; 31: iStockphoto

No part of this publication may be reproduced, stored in a retrieval system, or transmitted in any form or by any means, electronic, mechanical, photocopying, recording, or otherwise, without written permission of the publisher. For information regarding permission, write to Scholastic Inc., Attention: Permissions Department, 557 Broadway, New York, NY 10012.

ISBN 978-0-545-53238-9

Copyright © 2013 by Scholastic Inc.

All rights reserved. Published by Scholastic Inc. SCHOLASTIC and associated logos are trademarks and/or registered trademarks of Scholastic Inc.

12 11 10 9 8 7 6 5 4 3   13 14 15 16 17 18/0

Printed in the U.S.A   40
First printing, January 2013

Animals come in all shapes and sizes. In this book you'll meet some of the smallest and cutest animals around. Some you may know, and some you may never have heard of at all. But each of these little guys has one thing in common—they are all itty-bitty animals!

PYGMY HEDGEHOG

A full-grown pygmy hedgehog is about six to eight inches from its nose to its tail. They only weigh about one pound—that's smaller than a football! As a baby, a pygmy hedgehog is so small that it can fit on a spoon!

FENNEC FOX

The fennec fox is tinier than any other dog, wolf, fox, or coyote in the world. Its body may be small, but its ears are very big. In fact, for its size, its ears are larger than any other fox's. In some parts of the world, kids get to keep these furry friends as pets!

KITTI'S HOGNOSED BAT

This night flyer got its name because it has the body of a bat and the nose of a pig. Also known as a "bumblebee bat," it's about the same size as the buzzing **insect**. From one wing to the other wing measures less than two inches long, which makes it one of the smallest **mammals** in the world!

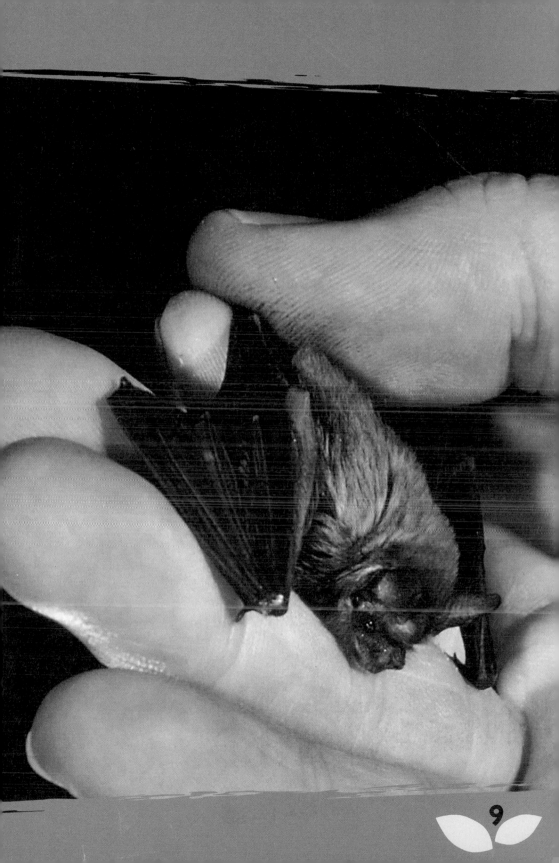

NORTHERN PYGMY OWL

The Northern Pygmy Owl can be found near coastlines and at forest edges all across North and Central America. It weighs two and a half ounces, which is about the size of a chicken's egg. It's different from other American owls because it's much smaller and not **nocturnal**.

HOO

PANDA COW

This cute creature is not a mix between a panda and a cow, but it sure looks like one! Instead, it is a special type of cow, with only twenty-five living in the world. Because they are so rare, they are sold to animal lovers all over the planet for more than $25,000.

MOOOOOOO

ASIAN SMALL-CLAWED OTTER

An Asian small-clawed otter is twenty-six to thirty-seven inches tall, and weighs between two and eleven pounds. It is the smallest **species** of otter in the world. Its claws may be small, but it can still use them to grab crabs, mussels, frogs, and snails to eat for dinner.

JERBOA

This jumping rodent is known for its large ears and small body. In fact, its ears are two-thirds the size of its body. This would be like an average-sized human having three-foot ears!

CUVIER'S DWARF CAIMAN

Crocodiles aren't known for being cuddly, but a Cuvier's dwarf caiman is the cutest croc around! A baby caiman is only a few inches long at birth. An adult caiman can grow to about four feet long, which may be the reason why some people like them as pets. Beware, though—they'll eat birds, fish, **reptiles**, mammals, and anything else they can get their teeth on!

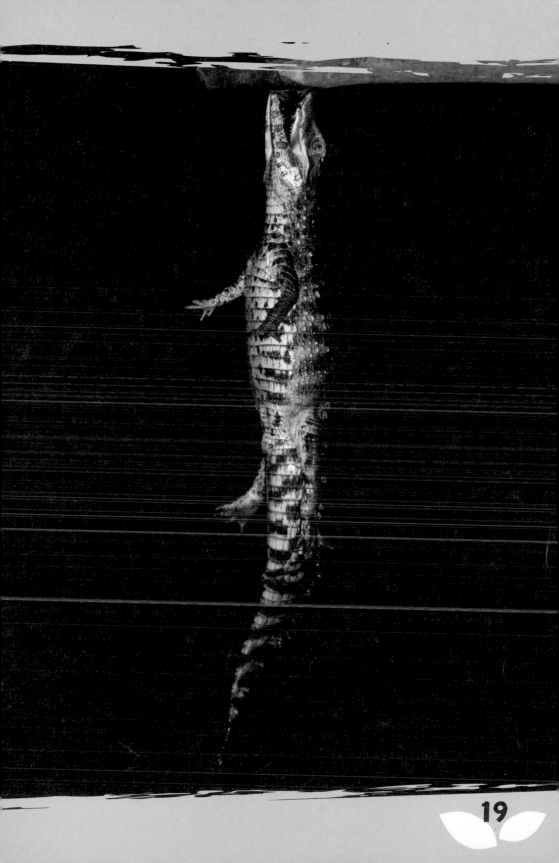

OLDE ENGLISH BABYDOLL SOUTHDOWN SHEEP

An Olde English Babydoll Southdown sheep is the tiniest type of sheep. They make great pets because of their small size and soft fur. They are so smart that they can even be taught to walk on a leash like a dog!

PYGMY HOG

A pygmy hog is the smallest and rarest species of wild pig. They stand ten to twelve inches high and can weigh up to twenty pounds. For a long time, they were believed to be **extinct**, but now we know there are about 100 to 200 still living in the wild.

BEYONCÉ

This tiny puppy was named after the superstar singer Beyoncé, and this year she might become almost as famous. The dachshund-mix puppy competed for the title of "World's Smallest Dog" in 2012. At birth, she could fit on a spoon; at two weeks old, she was the size of a business card; and at four months, she was about as big as a toddler's shoe!

MINIATURE DONKEY

On average, a miniature donkey is thirty-two to thirty-four inches tall and weighs 200 to 300 pounds when fully grown. That might sound heavy, but it's less than half of what full-size donkeys weigh. A mini donkey's back is still very strong and they can even take kids for rides.

SAND CAT

The sand cat gets its name because it's found in the sands of the Sahara Desert. They weigh between four and eight pounds and can grow to be ten to twelve inches long, which make them the smallest cats in the wild. They are hard to study because their tiny feet do not leave paw prints . . . which makes it difficult to keep track of them!

PYGMY HIPPO

Hippos are known for being huge, but not these little guys! A pygmy hippo weighs between 430 and 550 pounds, which is less than half of what a standard hippopotamus weighs. Originally from West Africa, a pygmy hippo was given as a gift to President Calvin Coolidge in 1927, and now they are in zoos all around the United States.

GLOSSARY

Insect: A small animal with three pairs of legs, one or two pairs of wings, and three main parts to its body.

Mammals: A warm-blooded animal that has hair or fur and usually gives birth to live babies.

Nocturnal: Active at night.

Species: A group into which animals and plants are divided.

Reptiles: A cold-blooded animal that crawls across the ground or creeps on short legs.

Extinct: No longer found alive.